PAISLEY
PUBLIC LIBRARY
Central Library, High Street,
Telephone: 041-889 2360

HOUR

Monday, Tuesday,
Thursday and Friday
10 a.m. — 8 p.m.

Wednesday and Saturday
10 a.m. — 5 p.m.

FINES:—Fines for detention
will be charged according to
the bye-laws.

RENEWALS:—Period of loan
may be renewed if the book
required by another

DAMAGED   OR
-Readers are required
care of books issued
Loss or damage
de good and the
books   lost   or
be charged.

ue for return
e stamped on

T REMOVE
nce fine will
t

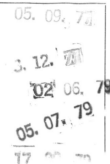

16825/71

ROME DONE LIGHTLY

ROME

DONE LIGHTLY

Drawings and Text by
GEORGE ADAMSON

1972
CHATTO & WINDUS
LONDON

Published by
Chatto & Windus Ltd
40 William IV Street
London W.C.2

*

Clarke, Irwin & Co. Ltd.
Toronto

ISBN 0 7011 1622 6

Printed in Great Britain by
Redwood Press Ltd.
Trowbridge, Wilts.

In Memory of Marie

....PERMESSO?

INTRODUCTION

ROME is a city to stroll in, and to think about, read about and dream about: which is a great deal to say of any place. It is rich in the detail and ideas of many centuries: it has cheerful, elegant people; a galaxy of ancient monuments, churches, palaces, galleries and museums, and many learned institutions and libraries; its haute couture and film studios have won international renown; it offers music and theatre, night clubs and illuminations. There are catacombs, parks, a zoo and a lido; an underground railway, a splendid railway station and an international airport; and, not least, good food, wine and water.

Without ostentation Rome offers this astonishing array to be experienced and remembered. Wouldn't you expect sometimes that impressions might become over-simplified – even a little mixed up?

OF the seven kings in Roman history it was the sixth, Servius Tullius, who set up a
new constitution and built a wall with nineteen gates round the seven hills. The

STAZIONE TERMINI, one of the best of Rome's modern buildings, incorporates part of that wall.

'THINK of it, Mabel–here stood John Milton, Edward Gibbon, Mendelssohn, Poussin, Berlioz, Mozart, Samuel Morse, Goethe, Princess Grace, Reynolds, Keats, Shelley, Alfred the Great, Pirandello, Wagner, Berenice, Turner, Thorwaldsen, Bonnie Prince Charlie, Dickens, Liszt, Corot, Ingres, Hans Andersen, the Kennedys, Mark Twain, Belloc, Evelyn, Casanova, Henry James, Rubens, Princess Margaret, Cantuar . . . and Mabel and Wilbur Clinton of Belleville, Ontario.'

Piazzas beckon

11

Fountains spurt

THE water comes from the ALBAN HILLS and is very good to drink. As you fill your plastic cup, think of San Filippo Neri's advice to the wives of Rome . . . if you can't speak mildly to your husband when he comes home, take a mouthful of water.

OPPOSITE: STEPS in Rome are sometimes the only means of reaching one district from another, but in a city built on seven hills this isn't surprising.

12

Steps climb

13

'ABSORBED by ceaseless invention and torn by multi-patronage, sometimes crafts-men would lose their way, forget precisely where they had been working, or die. So great was the activity of those days and so long postponed the settlement of fees, that sometimes lamentable omissions went unnoticed for centuries.' (Professor Everbold in his *Origin of the Bare Patches in Renaissance and Baroque Rome*.)

Conversation is visible

'MOLTO contento', 'ich möchte zahlen', 'e lei?', 'qu'a-t-il dit?', 'Let's all go to Livia's house', 'Preferisco Rococo', 'Salgo esta noche para . . .', 'Na zdrowie', 'Brutto', 'un' altra tazza', 'Basta!', '-ᴎᴀʀⴆ ıᴏᴎᴛᴀċ ᴀᴎ ʀⴑⴆ ᴀᴎ ꝓᴀ́ꝑᴀ ᴎᴀᴏṁᴛᴀ ᴀ ꝼᴇıᴄᴇᴀ́ʟ', 'Dywysog Cymru', '. . . it's next to Porta Pia' . . .

The pace can be leisurely

but Romans can hurry when they must

All roads lead to . . .

Against the skyline stone saints and fluttering bishops take on the threat of TV aerials

dark & wildly theatrically mmm

.... Seventeenth-century but underneath that it's ninth — and underneath that it's fourth. Again below, it's said to be the oldest in antiquity ...

JUST as the PALAZZO BARBERINI is the greatest secular Baroque building in Rome, so SAN DEMENTE holds its enviable position among the many churches. If you walk through to the adjoining monastery you may come across the monk who remembers with affection that great authority on Rome, Augustus Hare.

OPPOSITE:

THE top of this column reaches the height of the original ground level before the earth was removed — according to an inscription at the base of the column. Professor Everbold is convinced there may be other cases like this.

DI IMMORTALES!

A B C D E F G

from the base upwards the story of Emperor Trajan's campaigns is told for all to see..

..Isn't that our coach going?

CONSTANTINE began to build a basilica on this site in 324 A.D. It covered the tomb of St. Peter and it lasted more than twelve hundred years. The present SAN PIETRO was consecrated in 1626. Besides seeing the interior of this immense church and the Sacristy, Treasury, Crypt and even the underground tombs you can take a lift to the roof. When you've had an orange drink at the little bar, you can climb more than three hundred stairs in the double walls of the dome to reach the stone lantern on top. Don't lose your hat or your head.

A N Y city rich in architectural interest will have its visiting window-watchers, standing
in groups. But in the P IAZZA D I S AN P IETRO or at C ASTEL G ANDOLFO they stand
in crowds, looking up at a window, a hanging carpet, and eventually . . . *Il Papa.*

MOST Roman TERME (Baths) date from Imperial times when there were some twelve public baths and a considerable cult in their use. Besides the fine swimming pool of the FORO ITALICO, begun in 1931, there are now very many shower-baths, mostly in the hotels; any sign of cult is found only in those who know that *Apoditerium* is where you undress, and that *Frigidarium*, *Tepidarium* and *Calidarium* are rooms with bath-water of differing temperatures. *Tedium* is rare.

Harvesting —Corinthian capitals grow wild on the Palatine

TWO thousand seven hundred-odd years ago the legendary she-wolf suckled Romulus and Remus in a cave believed to be on the PALATINE HILL; and here Romulus ploughed his first furrow and built a wall. The original site of Rome has survived despite flames and sackings, whether occupied by hovel or imperial palace, by limeburners, monks or wilderness. In the sixteenth century the Farnese family levelled much of the ground to create their pleasure gardens; of course, in the eighteenth century it was picturesque with cattle; in the twentieth its wonderful ruins set amidst grass and trees were unearthed for the visitor to explore. You will even come across a simple bar *al fresco*.

Note the distant campanile of SANTA CATERINA FUORI DI MODA.

what the barbarians didn't do the Barberini did

...mentioned by Suetonius

...Telemachus...

Sixtus the fifth perhaps,
or was it Quintus the sixth?...

IF all the bronze, wood, iron, marble, brick and stone that once completed this wonderful building were to return to their original position, some Roman palaces might look half-ruined and others would completely disappear.

Mum!

floodlit every night

guides hold up numbers
to show
where your party
has got to

according to Nibby

according to Tabby

FROM twelve noon until at least three-thirty p.m. most churches, apart from the largest basilicas, are closed. From one o'clock until at least three-thirty many museums and galleries are closed and shops are shut. If you are not taking a siesta you could be planning

I want you to see the wonderful floor designed by Giovannino de' Dolci for the Sistine chapel.

to see some of the frescoes which abound: Republican, Imperial, early Christian, **Byzan**-tine and Renaissance, including the paintings in the SISTINE CHAPEL, NICHOLAS V's CHAPEL by Fra Angelico, and the STANZE of Raphael.

THIS MOSES, five minutes from the FORUM, in the ancient church of SAN PIETRO IN VINCOLI, was conceived by the sculptor Michelangelo as part of a monument for Julius II. It was never used.

...MOSES

THIS MOSES, five minutes from the STAZIONE TERMINI, in the ACQUA FELICE fountain, was conceived by the sculptor Bresciano as part of a monument for Sixtus V. It was never liked.

A CITY couldn't be as old as Rome is without its share of curious things – the ancient PONTE FABRICIO, popularly called the Ponte dei Quattro Capi, over the Tiber to the island ISOLA TIBERINA, is typical. Professor Everbold's latest find throws new light on the design practice of the architects of Imperial Rome. It is thought to have formed part of the floor of a municipal drawing office or of the house of a clerk of works; and it is called the mosaic of the Triumphal Arch.

No visit is complete that has missed the city's unequalled collection of holes, dating from ancient pagan times. You will easily recognise these cool and fascinating places, on the very edge of history, for they are always most carefully protected from damage by lattice fencing. Looking into them you may occasionally see the glow of an electric bulb, and just pick out some dusty archaeologist rinsing fragments of cut stone in a bowl of water. But most often you will only see velvet darkness and whatever is in your mind's eye.

la lista per favore...

O NE of the delights of Rome is *la cucina Romana*—the food and wine. You may find a tiny garden to sit in at a trattoria, or there may be a view of a floodlit piazza while you eat and listen to *canzoni romane* accompanied on concertina and mandolin. The piazza

Piazza Navona
Illuminata · Roma.

may have been used for horse-racing, for processions, for fireworks–or flooded with
water for naval spectacles in some Roman carnival of the past.

33

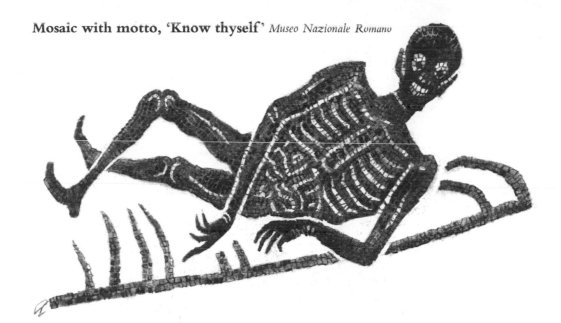

Mosaic with motto, 'Know thyself' *Museo Nazionale Romano*

'How I'd like some saltimbocca, bocca!'

'Ah, you've left it too late . . . that's the truth.'

Bocca della verità; the mouth of truth

Santa Maria in Cosmedin

IN the sixteenth century a Roman tailor named Pasquino voiced critical opinion about affairs to his customers. When he died the statue of Menelaus near his shop was renamed after him. Satirical notices were hung on it and caustic dialogues were written for this 'Pasquino' and the statue of Marforio—the first pasquinades. Other statues began to talk soon after.

WHEN it's hot and sunny your table-cloth is kept in place with the help of *acqua vergine*. What a use for such perfect drinking water!

OPPOSITE: AT Tivoli, in the hillside gardens of the Villa d'Este you mustn't drink the water as if you were in Rome. Just enjoy seeing all the things that exuberant Renaissance imagination found to do with it; and think of the story of Cardinal Gianni–how, shortly before he became Clement XVII, he substituted the well-known San Demente designs of the young Borromaserati for those of the aged and renowned Bornamante– as a revenge on the old man for a playfully-contrived squirt of water aimed up the Cardinal's soutane during a visit there.

Sunt lacrimae rerum, Abbé LISZT...

ACQVA
NON
POTABILE

Exactement, Monsieur FRAGONARD...

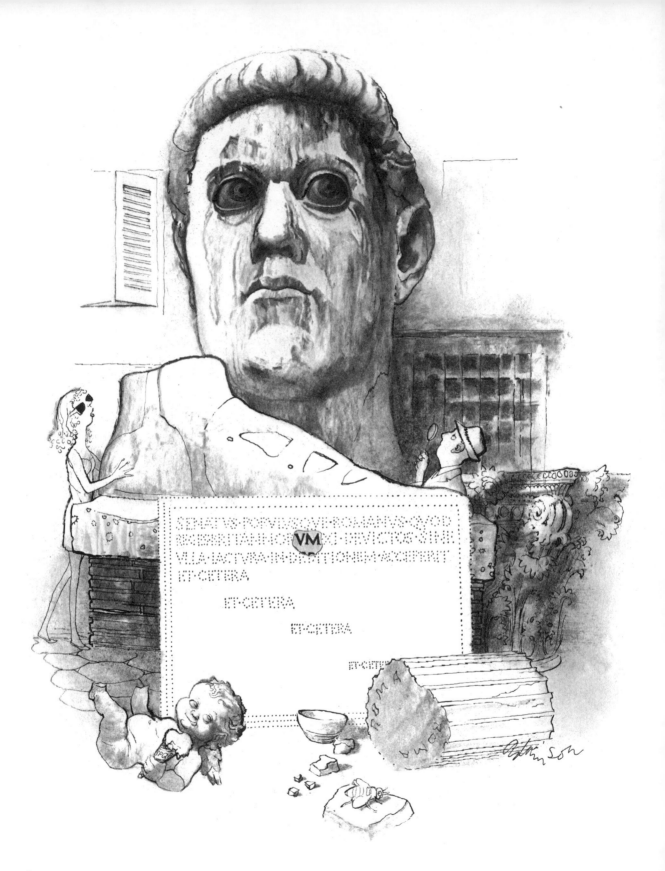

HALF an hour's ride by the *Metropolitana* and you are in OSTIA ANTICA. Here, as you walk about, you can imagine the day-to-day life of imperial and republican Romans. Excavations and restorations show their capitol, forum, tombs, temples, synagogue, theatre, baths, offices, homes, shops and storehouses. This was Rome's first colony: her seaport, military and commercial.

OPPOSITE: IN the most unexpected corners, instead of running water and plants, you often find Roman fragments. Some are of heroic proportions, others are no bigger than your hand. Fragments of columns, of statues, of inscriptions, all silently challenge the expert in you–can you visualise how the piece in front of you fitted some forgotten original? 'So little evidence, so much to say'–to quote from Professor Everbold's projected report for *Italia Nostra*.

SUMMER rain in Rome is an affront – and on Mondays it is quite unbearable, at least for visitors, as most museums are closed. But, *pazienza*! You are, after all, in the PIAZZA DEL CAMPIDOGLIO or CAPITOL: the very heart of Rome. It is still the seat of Rome's municipality, and best approached by the gentle ramp known as 'La Cordonata', part of Michelangelo's scheme. The central building with medieval towers is the

piano. piano !

PALAZZO DEL SENATORE, built over the TABULARIUM or Record Office: it is flanked by two fine museums. Near-by is the church of SANTA MARIA D'ARACOELI, on the site of Rome's first pagan temple. From the TABULARIUM erected by General Catulus in 78 B.C.–there is an excellent view of the FORUM.

41

THERE are few department stores in Rome, and shops of a kind tend to cluster together within a district: the *bottigliere* for wines, the delicatessen, gift shops and those selling statues, leather goods, pottery, raffia baskets, linens, woollens, hand-made shirts, shoes, jewellery, prints and antiques—and street bookstalls and umbrella stalls as well. And, of course, you can always enjoy the gentle delights of window shopping.

The magazine *This Week in Rome*, sold on the bookstalls, gives information on events and museum hours, etc. The *Rome Daily American* also gives details of events in the city. Interesting books include: Bowen, Elizabeth, *A Time in Rome* (London, 1960); Calza-Becatti, *Ostia* (Rome, 1965); Cooper, Gordon, *A Fortnight in Rome* (London, 1962); Hare, Augustus, *Walks in Rome* (London, 1867); Lugli, G., *The Roman Forum and the Palatine* (Rome, 1961); Masson, Georgina, *The Companion Guide to Rome* (London, 1965); Morton, H. V., *A Traveller in Rome* (London, 1957); Naval, Margret, *Rome Off the Record* (Vienna, 1960); Paglia, V., *What to See in Rome and its Environs* (Geneva); C. Galassi Paluzzi, *English Memories in Rome*–No. 2 of the collection 'Foreign Memories in Rome' (Rome, 1964); Rowdon, M., *A Roman Street* (London, 1964).

Napoleon Bonaparte's sister, *Galleria Borghese*

ACKNOWLEDGEMENTS

My thanks are due to: the British Museum and the Mansell Collection for photographs on pp. 8-9 appearing l. to r. as follows: Capitoline Venus (Mansell), Hadrian (B.M.), Vestal Virgin (Mansell), Diocletian (Mansell), Nero (Mansell), Augustus Caesar (Mansell), Antonia, Mother of Claudius (B.M.), Greek Apollo (B.M.), Trajan (B.M.); the Italian Institute and the Italian State Tourist Office, London, and the Ente Provinciale per il Turismo, Rome, for their help; the proprietors of *Punch* for permission to use the drawings on pp. 11-19, and also those on pp. 22 and 23; the proprietors of *Time and Tide* for permission to use the drawing on p. 5; Mrs. M. V. Constable, B.A., B.Litt., and several friends for valuable help; to my wife for all her good advice, and constant encouragement, and to my sons, especially for their work in Rome.